Kim's Choice

Brigit Viney

Easystart

Series Editors: Andy Hopkins and Jocelyn Potter

1.1 What's the book about?

Look at the pictures on pages 1 and 2.

1 What do you know about Kim? Write *Yes, No* or *?*.

a Kim is a student. ....*Yes*............

b Kim plays football. ....

c Kim is a good runner. ....

d Girls and boys run with Kim. ....

e Kim has light hair. ....

f Kim is about twelve years old. ....

2 Who are these people? Write the words from the box under the right picture.

> father happy at school man teacher woman at home angry

....*father*....

....

....

....

....

....

....

....

1.2 What happens next?

What do you think? Circle your answers.

1 Kim *runs* / *doesn't run* for her school.

2 Kim's father *isn't* / *is* happy with Kim.

3 Kim *doesn't go* / *goes* shopping at the weekend.

4 Kim *meets some* / *doesn't meet any* new people.

5 Kim *doesn't go* / *goes* to some places with her father.

'One, two, three, go!' Mrs Evans says.

Four girls – Laura, Sarah, Deborah and Kim – run a hundred **metre**s. Kim finishes first.

'Good,' Mrs Evans says to Kim. 'You run very well. Can you run for the school later this summer?'

choice /tʃɔɪs/ (n) Blue or green – is that the *choice* of colour?
metre /ˈmiːtə/ (n) My father is two *metres* tall.

'Oh, yes, please!' Kim answers. She is twelve, and this is her first year at this school.

That evening Kim asks her father, 'Can I go to Allen's Athletics **Club** on Saturday?'

Her father looks at her. 'This is new!' he says. 'OK, you can go.'

club /klʌb/ (n) Children come to the *club* and play after school.

On Saturday morning Kim and her father go to the club and meet the **coach**. He smiles and says, 'Hello, Kim. Come with me!'

They go to the **track**. Some children are there. Kim and the children run slowly for twenty **minute**s and then they **stretch** for twenty minutes. After this, they run fifty metres quickly. They run quickly again – and again. Then they run slowly for ten minutes.

coach /kəʊtʃ/ (n) He works in an office but at weekends he is a football *coach*.
track /træk/ (n) The new *track* is open and I run there.
minute /ˈmɪnɪt/ (n) She only waits five *minutes*. Then she goes away.
stretch /stretʃ/ (v) I *stretch* and then I get up.

Kim's father asks, 'Do you like it here?'

'Yes!' Kim answers.

Kim's father takes her to the athletics club every week. He watches her. 'She's very good,' he thinks.

There are often **race**s at the club and sometimes Kim **win**s them. Her father is happy then.

After six weeks the coach says, 'There's a **competition** at Barton Athletics Club on Saturday. Can you go? Ask your mother and father.'

That afternoon Kim talks to her mother and father about the competition. Her friend Hannah is there.

'Come shopping with me on Saturday!' Hannah says.

'Competitions are very important,' Kim's father says.

'Sorry, Hannah,' Kim says.

race /reɪs/ (n) Every year there is a bicycle *race* across the town.
win /wɪn/ (v) We *win* every game.
competition /ˌkɒmpəˈtɪʃən/ (n) This is my story for the *competition* in the newspaper.

On Saturday Kim's father drives her to the competition. There are children there from Barton Athletics Club.

Kim's first race is at ten o'clock. One girl is tall and strong. Kim looks at her. Suddenly, Kim hears the **gun**. The tall girl starts quickly. She wins, and Kim is **third**.

gun /gʌn/ (n) The man has a *gun*! Run!
third /θɜːd/ (adj) I like two of the bedrooms, but the *third* bedroom is very small.

The **second** race is at twelve o'clock. The tall girl is there again – and again she wins.

In the third race Kim starts very quickly, and she wins. She is very happy. Her father says, 'Good girl!'

second /ˈsekənd/ (adj) His first film is good, but I don't like his *second* film.

7

2.1 Were you right?

Look at your answers to Activity 1.2 on page ii. What comes first? And then? Write the numbers, 1–6.

◯ Kim wins some races at the club.

◯ The tall girl from Barton Athletics Club wins two races and Kim wins one race.

1 Mrs Evans asks, 'Kim, can you run for the school later this summer?'

◯ Kim's father drives her to a competition.

◯ Kim meets the coach and some runners at Allen's Athletics Club.

◯ Kim makes a choice about shopping with Hannah.

2.2 What more did you learn?

1 Circle the right answer.

a Laura, Sarah, Deborah and Kim *run* / *swim* / *drive* a hundred *days* / *minutes* / *metres.*

b Mrs Evans thinks, 'Kim runs very *slowly* / *well* / *quietly.*'

c This is Kim's *first* / *second* / *third* year at Mrs Evans's school.

d At the athletics club, Kim goes to the *school* / *cinema* / *track* with *her mother* / *the athletics coach* / *the music teacher.*

e At the track, Kim and the children *dance and play* / *run and stretch* / *talk and eat.*

2 Match the words in *italics* with words in the box.

a Kim goes to Allen's Club with *him* every week. ·····

b *She* is Kim's friend.

c *She* works at Kim's school.

d *He* works at Allen's Athletics Club.

e Allen's Athletics Club is for *them.*

| Kim's coach |
| Hannah |
| Kim's father |
| runners |
| Mrs Evans |

8

2.3 Language in use

Look at the sentence in the box. Then read the story. Circle the right words.

> Can I go **to** Allen's Athletics Club **on** Saturday?

Many children go (**a**) *to* / *at* / *in* Allen's Athletics Club (**b**) *in* / *at* / *on* Saturdays. They come (**c**) *from* / *for* / *about* many schools (**d**) *on* / *in* / *at* Kim's town.

The coach always talks (**e**) *at* / *to* / *from* them (**f**) *about* / *for* / *with* athletics. The boys and girls listen (**g**) *about* / *a* / *to* him. He is a good coach. The children work well (**h**) *at* / *from* / *to* the club.

First, they usually run slowly. Then they stretch (**i**) *for* / *at* / *on* twenty minutes. Then they run quickly. The coach quietly looks (**j**) *to* / *at* / *with* the runners.

Later the coach talks (**k**) *for* / *about* / *to* a boy and two girls (**l**) *about* / *in* / *for* a big race. 'Can you run (**m**) *in* / *for* / *to* the club?' he asks them. 'Can you go (**n**) *to* / *with* / *in* a competition (**o**) *at* / *about* / *with* me (**p**) *for* / *on* / *at* Tuesday (**q**) *on* / *at* / *in* two o'clock?'

The children are very happy. They say, 'Yes, please!'

2.4 What's next?

Kim is a good runner. Are Kim's competitions very important to Kim, her family and her friends? What do you think? Write *always* or *sometimes*.

1 Kim   ....

2 Kim's mother   ....

3 Kim's father   ....

4 Kim's coach   ....

5 Kim's friends   ....

At home Kim talks about the competition. 'That tall girl – Nicole
– is very good.'

'You can be very good too!' her father says.

'Perhaps,' her mother says. 'But school is important.'

'OK,' Kim says. 'I can run for the school too.'

'When can you run for the school?' her father asks.

'George, stop,' her mother says. 'Time for bed, Kim.'

In July Kim runs for her school in an important competition, but she doesn't win. Her father isn't happy, but he says, 'You're a good **runner**. **Train**, and you can win every competition. You can be famous.'

In the winter there aren't any competitions, but Kim trains at the club every week. Her father always goes with her. Sometimes he is ill, but he always goes.

For three years Kim trains two or three times every week. She wins competitions at school and with the club, and she gets some beautiful **trophies**. There are photos of her in the newspaper.

runner /ˈrʌnə/ (n) There are only four *runners*. Can I run too?
train /treɪn/ (v) The footballers *train* every morning and every evening.
trophy /ˈtrəʊfi/ (n) England play well, but the *trophy* often goes to New Zealand.

Kim's father loves the trophies and photos. But sometimes Kim thinks, 'I never go out with my friends. I only go to the club with my father.'

Then Kim has a difficult year at school. She is sixteen and she has important **exam**s in the summer. She wants some time with her friends too.

'I can only train on one evening,' she says to her father.

'The competitions this year are very important. Go to the club two or three evenings,' he answers.

exam /ɪgˈzæm/ (n) The students have *exams* this week.

But Kim doesn't listen to him.

Kim doesn't only think about exams and her friends. There is a new boy at school. His name is Curtis and he has beautiful brown eyes and a big smile.

'Does he have a girlfriend?'
Kim asks Hannah.

'I don't know. Ask him,'
Hannah says. But Kim can't.

'Can I ask him for you?'
Hannah asks.

'No!' Kim says.

3.1 Right or wrong?

Look at your answers to Activity 2.4 on page 9. Who is talking in the sentences here?

1 'But school is important.'   ....._Kim's mother_.....

2 'You can be famous.'   ....

3 'I never go out with my friends.'   ....

4 'I can only train on one evening.' ....

5 'Go to the club two or three evenings.' ....

6 'Does he have a girlfriend?'   ....

7 'Can I ask him for you?'   ....

3.2 What more did you learn?

Are the sentences right (✓) or wrong (✗)?

1 Nicole is short.   ✗

2 She is a good runner.

3 Kim's mother never thinks about her daughter's problems.

4 George is Kim's coach.

5 For him, exams are very important for Kim.

6 He likes athletics trophies.

7 Curtis is a new boy at Kim's school.

8 He has brown eyes.

9 Hannah is Kim's good friend.

10 She is a runner.

11 Kim runs for the school and the club.

12 Her picture is never in the newspaper.

3.3 Language in use

Look at the sentences in the box. Then finish
the second sentences with one or two words.

> Nicole is **a tall** girl.
>
> Sometimes he is **ill**.

1 Kim's father says, 'You are a **good** runner.'
   He says, 'You are .... *good* ....'
2 In July Kim has **an important** competition.
   The competition in July is ....
3 Kim's father thinks, 'Kim can be **famous**.'
   He thinks, 'Kim can be .... runner.'
4 Sometimes he isn't **a happy** man.
   Sometimes he isn't ....
5 Kim has **some beautiful** trophies.
   Kim's trophies are ....
6 Kim has **a difficult** year at school and **some important** exams in the
   summer.
   Kim's year at school is .... and her exams are

   ....

7 Curtis's eyes are **beautiful and brown** and his smile is **big**.
   He has .... eyes and .... smile.

3.4 What's next?

What do you think? Circle the right answers.

1 Kim's mother talks to her about ... .
   a her schoolwork
   b athletics
2 Kim ... to Curtis.
   a talks
   b doesn't talk
3 Curtis is ... .
   a Hannah's boyfriend
   b Kim's boyfriend
4 Kim's father takes photographs of ... .
   a the family on holiday
   b Kim with her trophies

5 In June Kim's father is ... with
   Kim at the competition.
   a happy
   b unhappy
6 Kim ... in her exams.
   a does well
   b doesn't do well
7 Kim ... a famous runner.
   a is
   b isn't

15

One evening at the club the coach says, 'There's an important competition on June 30th, Kim. Can you go?' 'Yes,' she answers. 'School finishes on the 15th.'

'Good,' the coach says. 'You can win this competition!'

Then two days later Curtis suddenly asks her, 'Can you come to the school **disco** with me?'

'Yes!' Kim answers.

disco /'dɪskəʊ/ (n) They go to the *disco* and dance all night.

'When is the disco?' Kim asks Curtis.

'Friday, 29th,' Curtis says.

'The day before my competition ...'

'Is that a problem?'

'No, no!' she answers.

At home her father is angry. 'You can't go to the disco. You can't run well after a late night,' he says.

It is June 29th. Kim is putting on a long red dress.

'Go to the disco, and you can't come back!' her father says. He is very angry.

Kim puts some **clothes** in a bag. 'I'm going,' she says.

She dances all night with Curtis. She has a good time, but she is angry with her father. She stays the night with Hannah.

clothes /kləʊðz, kləʊz/ (n pl) Let's buy some new *clothes* for our holiday.

Kim goes to the competition. Her father doesn't go with her. She doesn't win, but she isn't unhappy. She doesn't go home again, and she doesn't go to the **athletics** club.

'I'm not a runner now,' she says to Curtis.

At home the house is quiet. Her father doesn't talk about her, but he looks at her trophies and photos every day. 'Come back,' he thinks. 'You can be famous.'

athletics /æθ'letɪks, əθ-/ (n) I can't run quickly but I like *athletics*.

Look at the box. Then read the sentences and write the numbers, 1–5. Talk to your friends about your choice of numbers.

| 1 Very unhappy | 2 Unhappy | 3 OK | 4 Happy | 5 Very happy |

○ a **Kim's coach at the club.** Kim says, 'I can go to the competition on June 30th.'

○ b **Kim at school.** Curtis says, 'Can you come to the school disco with me?'

○ c **Curtis at school.** Kim says, 'Yes! I can go to the disco with you.'

○ d **Kim's father at home.** Kim goes to the school disco.

○ e **Kim and Curtis at school.** At the school disco.

○ f **Kim at Hannah's house.** After the school disco.

○ g **Kim at the athletics competition.** On June 30th after her race.

○ h **Kim's father at home.** On July 1st.

Write about it

You are Kim. Write about your day.

My ....coach.... at Allen's Athletics Club says, 'You are a good .... Can you come to an important .... on June 30th?' My .... says, 'You can .... the competition. Go to the .... two or three times every ....' But I can't go to the club two or three times every week. I have important .... in the summer. And now I have a new friend. His .... is Curtis, and he has beautiful .... and a big .... Competitions are not very important to me now. There is a .... at school on June 29th. Curtis says, 'Can you come to the disco with me?' I am very .... ! But then my father says, 'You can't go to the disco on .... 29th. You have a .... on June 30th.'

1 **Talk to your friends about the problems of young people. Talk about the questions.**

a   Who do young people have problems with?

Notes

b   What problems do they have with the people in **a**?

Notes

2 **Read the letter and write an answer.**

I am an unhappy 14-year-old girl at a new school.

I walk to school every day at 8 o'clock. On the street I see students from my school. I say, 'Hello.' But they don't say, 'Hi.' They don't walk with me.

At school no students sit near me. They listen to the teacher. They eat at 1 o'clock. They play games – but they don't talk to me.

After school I go home. I watch TV and read a book. But I don't telephone my friends. I don't go to a club. I don't have any friends.

What can I do?   The New Girl

Dear New Girl